The Doctrine of Karate

by
James D. Brumbaugh

Dedication

This paper is dedicated to all the sensei who helped me along my karate journey and to all those who will come after me on their own journey, both my students and those who are training under someone else. Karate is a personal journey that can last a lifetime. I hope the discussion within this work will spur others to think about the fabric holding karate together.

Included are three related essays, "Doctrine, Strategy, Tactics: Who Cares" and "Styles: Marketing Tool or the Foundation for Learning?" and "The Mind and the Martial Artist."

I hope readers will find these writings thought provoking.

Introduction

What is karate? What is the basis for it as a martial art of self-defense? These questions are repeated over and over in dojo around this country. Often the answers are unsatisfactory. Students want knowledge, and yet the truth is not easy to pin down. On the surface, karate appears to be a simple art that involves punching and kicking. It seems to be about learning unique mechanical motions called techniques. As students train and learn more than the basics, what seemed simple begins to take on a complex nature. The more complex it becomes, the more perplexing the true nature of karate appears. As the karateka advances, similarities to other martial arts are observed. Asking questions about karate's roots and trying to trace the history of the art only leads to more confusion. The history of karate seems irrevocably intertwined with other martial arts so much so that the demarcation between arts has been lost, if it ever concisely existed. The more one searches for clear-cut answers, the more the question becomes whether karate ever actually existed as a separate entity.

And yet there is something unique about karate, something distinct. There is a different "feel" to it. When did karate separate from other arts and why? If karate does exist as a separate art, then there must be a distinctive foundation of general, underlying principles that provide the groundwork for the art. So, how can these principles be discovered? Searching the literature for clues to the nature of karate reveals no simple answers. The principles that guided the founders are vague or unrecorded. Despite the confusing and contradictory information found in most of the literature, it is possible to reach certain conclusions by extrapolating.

Karate is generally accepted as an antique martial art that was formulated, or translated from, various Chinese martial styles of chuan-fa through a few Okinawans who blended the Chinese styles with the Okinawan art *te* sometime between the late 1700s to early 1900s. It is also generally accepted that karate was initially a self-defense, either for palace guards as suggested by Choki Motobu[1] or for the nobility as suggested by Mark Bishop[2] or even for the general populace as suggested by Peter Lewis.[3] The best-known early masters studied chuan-fa by traveling to China personally or from Chinese practitioners who visited Okinawa. While in the case of the earliest Okinawan masters there is sometimes confusion as to the exact details of their training, it is apparent that the roots of the martial arts they practiced are traceable to China. One such example is Sakugawa, one of the most important early karateka. Depending on the source, he was reported to have either traveled to China to learn Chinese boxing[4] or he learned it on Okinawa[5]. Kanryo Higaonna, another important figure in Okinawan karate, is reported to have done both, learning from experts in Okinawa and visiting China to further his training and knowledge.[6] If so many of the early masters who were instrumental in the formation of karate trained in chuan-fa, then when and how did these Chinese systems become karate?

Simply identifying its origin is not enough to define karate since the art has certainly not been static. In the last seventy-five years, karate has evolved beyond the status of a little-known yet practical self-defense, into a way for self-refinement (*do*), a sport, and now into various fitness/conditioning programs. The relation between karate and self-defense has blurred to the extent that many respected karateka are asking if karate as it is now taught contains the necessary elements of a useful self-defense. Vince Morris notes in the preface to his book on kyusho-jutsu that there was "the proliferation of Japanese-centered styles post World War Two which concentrated on developing and promoting the newly emerging sporting aspects of karate with little attention to, nor knowledge of, the more profound and dangerous non-sporting, self-defence constituents."[7] Many authors feel this transition away from karate as a self-defense was initiated at the beginning of the 19th century by Ankoh Itosu. A. S. Rench suggests, "By the late 1930s, the majority of karate practiced was stripped of its dangerous and combat-effective techniques. Most of what remained was reduced to a form of cultural recreation."[8]

The more karate is scrutinized, the more questions arise that go unanswered. To seek answers to all of them goes far beyond the scope of this analysis. Instead, an attempt to explore and understand the roots of karate as a system of self-defense will be made. At the same time, the significance of other important variations of karate will not be overlooked. To understand karate more fully, it is necessary to search for the underlying principles that set karate apart from other methods of self-defense. For simplicity, the term *doctrine* will be used to mean these fundamental principles. Therefore, the question this paper intends to answer is: What is the doctrine on which karate was built?

It is important to differentiate between *doctrine* and two other terms that are commonly applied to any martial art and are often used mistakenly as synonymous for doctrine. Those two terms are *strategy* and *tactics*. For the purposes of this paper, we will use the definitions arrived at in the author's earlier paper "Doctrine, Strategy, Tactics: Who Cares?" published in the United States Karate Association Forum, December, 1996 and included here as Appendix A. As defined in that paper, <u>*doctrine* is the general principles and philosophy that provides the framework within which a martial art functions.</u> <u>*Doctrine* establishes the theory of combat that dictates the methods a martial art will use.</u> <u>*Doctrine* dictates the tools that will be used for any given martial art</u>. This definition is generally in agreement with doctrine as defined by Morgan in his book *Living the Martial Way.*[9]

Strategy is the theoretical analysis of possible opponents using the principles set forth in the doctrine and planning the best self-defense applications against those opponents. <u>*Strategy* consists of the plans for actual use in combat of the tools dictated by the doctrine.</u> *Strategy* may be offensive or defensive. Strategies will be devised to cover as many enemies as possible by examining possible weakness and strengths. *Strategy* is the plan that connects doctrine and tactics.

<u>*Tactics* are intelligent acts of combat performed during aggressive confrontation that fulfill the principles of doctrine and the plans of strategy.</u> *Tactics* are the physical application of the plans and principles of a martial art. *Tactics* convert the theory and plans from doctrine and strategy into actions. *Tactics* provide a way for the mind to guide the body in actual self-defense situations to increase the likelihood of success

(success in simplest terms being survival). *Tactics* are the physical "doing".

In general, tactics and strategy are not relevant to this paper. However, in those areas where doctrine and strategy are often confused, some clarification will be attempted. It is also possible for strategy and tactics to exist in situations where no doctrine has been established. One example of the recently developed eclectic styles without a doctrine is Jeet Kune Do. Here there are no classical standards and the pervading belief is that anything that works is acceptable.[10] Doctrine is deemed unnecessary. Changes that occur continually are solely dependent on the current focus of the practitioner. Many modern styles, especially in the west, have such a basis since the general driving force to create the style in the first place is economic. As ideas come to mind, the founder adds or subtracts as the mood (market) dictates. Thus, training methods seem to be always changing and there does not appear to be a unifying set of principles. These types of systems will not be studied here.

To further explain the terminology and application of doctrine, strategy and tactics, carpentry might be used as analogous in the sense that it is a "construction art." The *doctrine* for the art of carpentry could be to build structures using wood, hammer, rule, level, nail, saw, etc. This immediately differentiates carpentry from plumbing, bricklaying, or other construction arts. *Strategy* then is the summation of the methods used to plan, measure, secure, and generally perform carpentry tasks. *Tactics* are the actual sawing, nailing, and building of a structure.

To establish a probable doctrine for karate it is imperative to first define what characterizes karate. Since, as noted earlier, karate has evolved over the years, any definition of karate must include both what karate is and when it was created. A simple definition of karate might be that it is an ancient art of unarmed self-defense. This is what beginners are taught. But what makes it different from other martial arts? Subjectively, there is an underlying "feeling" of what karate is. Martial artists refer to themselves as *karateka* or *Tae Kwan Do* practitioners. They use the terms as if to identify themselves as students of separate martial arts without explaining the difference.

Through common usage karate has come to mean almost any self-defense system that includes some degree of hitting, striking or kicking. Many schools advertise that they teach karate without presenting a clear definition of what it is they teach. In various situations, the term karate may refer to Okinawan, Japanese, Korean, or Hawaiian striking arts, various jujutsu schools, and judo reformulated as self-defense. Additionally, karate often includes portions of kobudo. If there ever was a precise definition for the term "karate" it seems to have disappeared. For karate to be a distinctive martial art it cannot be all things to all people. Therefore, this paper will also attempt to answer the question: How can karate be concisely defined?

Before undertaking the search for a definition of karate, the term impact (or percussion) technique must be understood. As used within this paper, impact techniques are defined as "to hit or strike by projecting a portion of the body forcefully at an opponent so that the force of contact produces damage to the opponent". This contrasts with grappling which includes grabbing, holding, joint-bending and choking. The terms "impact technique" and "percussion technique" will be used interchangeably.

In addition, there are, several different manifestations of karate whose existence leads to questions about whether they are similar enough to have the same doctrine, or so dissimilar as to have been formulated using different doctrines. These include the *jutsu* or single-minded practice for combat effectiveness, the way (*do*) toward self-improvement, which developed out of the *jutsu* but has the goal of self-perfection, and the tournament application of karate. All of these variations of the art of karate seem to have legitimate claim to the name karate as a martial art yet all are different. Are they too different to all have the same doctrine?

Finally, as noted earlier, the history of karate is intertwined with other martial arts. Karate shares many techniques and strategies with other martial arts. Karate and all other weaponless martial arts share the same ultimate goal. So where does karate fit amongst the various weaponless martial arts?

The original question, what is the doctrine of karate, depends on answering several other questions. To summarize, this paper will attempt to answer the following questions: (1) How can karate be defined? (2) What is the doctrine or founding principles of karate? (3) Do the various manifestations of karate share a common doctrine? (4) Where does karate fit among the many different martial arts as a self-defense system? In discovering the answers to these questions several areas will be investigated. These include an examination of the time frame for the emergence of karate from its beginnings in chuan-fa and *te*, the differences between karate and other martial arts, and the differences between the actual doctrine for karate and strategies commonly presented as doctrines.

Discussion

As mentioned, the search for the doctrine of karate begins by attempting to define karate as a martial art. Investigation into this subject leads to some tenuous historical information since most "records" are more word-of-mouth myths than factually substantiated history.[11] Nonetheless, judicious examination of the literature can lead by extrapolation to some logical conclusions.

Breaking down the term martial art at the broadest level, there is: "martial" meaning something inclined or disposed toward war, and "art" meaning the principles or methods governing any craft or human activity. A martial art then is comprised of the principles governing a craft designed for use in warfare.

There are several levels on which the term "martial art" may be applied. There are martial arts applied by groups such as armies, or socio-political groups. And there are martial arts designed specifically for the individual. For both the group and the individual, the basic goal is survival. Appendix 1 illustrates the comparative hierarchy of the components of survival skills for both groups and individuals. From this it can be seen that karate is indeed a martial art concerned with individual survival.

Still, at this level, the concept is too broad to define distinctive martial arts. This definition includes Oriental and European arts, and everything from throwing grenades to all manner of unarmed combat. Depending on the dojo, style or head instructor, karate is taught as either an exclusively "empty hand" art or as a martial art that includes several weapon arts like bo, nunchaku, kama, etc. The use of weapons as an integral part of karate training only complicates the search for the doctrine of karate. Doctrines for arts using weapons are by the very presence of the weapon irreconcilably different from weaponless arts. If a weapon is at hand, the training includes the use of it. If there are no weapons, the art is formulated around what to do with only the body itself.

But why is it so important to train in a martial art that presupposes the combatant has no weapon? Some legends infer that the birth of "empty hand" self-defense was fostered by the Okinawan peasants when the weapons were taken away by legal decree. Generally, historians disagree with this oversimplification. Most peasants were too busy scratching out a living to have time to develop or master martial arts. Furthermore, systems of unarmed self-defense pre-date any documented Okinawan system. Even today, with the high degree of technology employed in combat, soldiers still learn and have a need for empty hand combat systems. In short, at the heart of the development of weaponless systems of combat is the sense of vulnerability every warrior feels when forced to defend himself without weapons. This vulnerability is reinforced by the very real probability that this type of situation could happen. And since every warrior realizes the potential of being forced into a violent confrontation when no weapons are available, either through loss or inoperative status, then a weaponless system of self-defense is required. Karate fills that need.

Karate indeed is a word derived from the Oriental ideographs (kanji or picture writing). The modern kanji for karate is made up of the two parts "kara" meaning "empty" and and "te" "hand". It is evident from this that the idea of self-defense without weapons was important to those who coined this name for karate. It is well documented that the early kanji for "karate" originated sometime in the 19th century and referred to "China hand", not "empty hand" as it is today.[12,13] At this point, it is not the term that is important but the evolutionary history of the martial art that became karate. Following this progression shows that originally the karate practiced on Okinawa was similar to the chuan-fa of China. The early use of a term meaning China hand demonstrates that the early Okinawan masters felt tied closely enough with China and the Chinese martial arts to refer to the Okinawan art as something from China. History shows that early masters did indeed practice Chinese self-defense and it was near the end of the 19th Century when changes began to formulate karate as a separate art. Nagamine suggests that the issue of the name given to the Okinawan martial art was settled once and for all at a meeting in 1936 between Miyagi, Hanashiro, Motobu, Kyan and others. At this meeting, it was decided by consensus to call the art "karate" meaning an "empty-handed self-defense art" or a "weaponless art of self-defense."[14] There can be little doubt that the need to develop a weaponless martial art and karate's preponderance of weaponless applications was one of the major factors compelling this highly respected group of masters to finally decide on the kanji for karate meaning "empty hand."

Therefore, having clearly established the importance of a weaponless art, and without further justification, it is concluded that karate, for the purposes of defining it and its doctrine, is a martial art applied by individuals who are without weapons. And since the doctrine for any weapon art will be significantly different from that for any weaponless art, the use of weapons will be excluded from this investigation.

But having established karate as a weaponless art only limits slightly what karate may be. In order to define karate, it is necessary to trace its history on a chronological basis. Included in this search are several important aspects of karate that have changed with the passage of time. These will be examined in order to establish the essence of the art. These include, but are not limited to, the name given to the art during various time periods, the important masters of those times, and descriptions of the art as those masters practiced it.

To establish a definition for karate, we begin by tracing the history of karate and its roots in China. History connects Chinese martial arts with Okinawa as far back as 1393 with the 36 families[15] but the transition from Chinese martial arts to karate came later. The earliest martial artist generally connected directly with the birth of karate is Tode Sakugawa. His life is reported as spanning either 1733-1815, 1762-1843, or 1774-1838 depending on the source.[16] As reported by McCarthy, Sakugawa, who was a security agent for at least part of his life, studied the fighting traditions in Fouzhou, Beijing and Satsuma. It is also reported that Sakugawa learned from the Chinese master Kusankun and that either he or Kusankun may have brought the *Bubishi* (a basic martial arts reference book) to Okinawa from China.[17] Regardless of the historical version of Sakugawa's training ascribed to, it is clear that Sakugawa was trained in China and was in fact a master of some form of chuan-fa. He was given the name *Tode*, which is the Okinawan reading of the characters originally used for karate, meaning

Tang (China) hand. Nagamine suggests that the term *tode* was used to distinguish the art practiced by certain Okinawans as being different from *te* which is the martial art known to have been indigenous to Okinawa.[18] By inference, Sakugawa was training in an art separate from *te* which they chose to call *tode* (or karate - China hand). Sakugawa, therefore, is the figure associated with the founding of a new art. McCarthy also points out that Sakugawa had a profound impact on self-defense methods that developed around Shuri. Shuri, as will be shown, is the well documented birthplace for numerous karate styles and masters. Haines reports that Sakugawa went to China in 1724 (contradicts dates above) and returned many years later to found the "now-famed Sakugawa school of karate" though the martial art taught there originally was most likely based on Chinese chuan-fa.[19] This reinforces the idea that Sakugawa was among the founders of what would become modern karate. To prove that *tode*, or Chinese self-defense, is the forerunner of karate it is necessary to trace the art from teacher to student. One way to do this is to start with Sakugawa and following the lineage of the masters through to the present thus formulating a historical understanding of karate.

Sakugawa, at least in some fashion, helped with the training of Sokon Matsumura who was a bodyguard to several Okinawan kings. Matsumura (1809 - 1901) also made trips to China where he studied under Chinese boxing experts Ason and Iwah[20]. Matsumura taught in Shuri, as did Sakugawa, and contributed heavily to passing *tode* from the early 19th century on to the late 19th century. Because of these strong connections to Chinese teachers, there is credence to the idea that at this time the martial art taught in Shuri remained strongly related to the Chinese methods. Up to this point, it may have been more a form of chuan-fa than modern karate.

Also teaching in Shuri during this general timeframe was master Ankoh Itosu (1813-1915 or 1832-1916), who more than any other late 19th century Okinawan master, reshaped karate into the art found at the end of World War II. Itosu studied under a number of teachers including Sokon Matsumura and a Chinese master living in Okinawa. Itosu began the reforms that eventually led to the introduction of karate to the Okinawan school system. Itosu is credited with the development of the five pinan kata. Some historians credit him with development of the corkscrew punch as it now exists.[21] Evidence reveals the corkscrew punch in several Chinese systems that pre-date karate and it even appears in the Eight Brocades, a Chinese exercise system dating as far back as 1100 A.D.

Nonetheless, Itosu was a primary force behind numerous changes to karate. As part of the reformation for use in the schools, Itosu removed many techniques that were judged too dangerous for use by children. Itosu is credited with teaching the idea that the body should be able to take blows and that karateka should not worry so much about mobility. This is a dramatic departure from the "light and airy" Chinese systems that were practiced by earlier masters. It is this change in basic strategy that can be seen in later karate due, no doubt, to the tremendous influence of Itosu's karate, if for no other reason than the numbers of school children who learned karate during their education.

At the same time, as the name for the martial art that was commonly practiced in Okinawa changed to karate (empty hand), various styles of the art begin to emerge. Instead of teaching karate as a general method for unarmed self-defense as had been done in the past, various masters began to sort out and separate according to distinctive styles. Early literature made little reference to specific styles. As McCarthy put it, "Sometime between 1784 and 1903, karate replaced *te* as the common term used to designate the major fighting forms of Okinawa. During the latter part of the 19th century the general classifications for various karate methods were named for the cities where they are practiced. The most important were Shuri-te (where Sakugawa and Matsumura taught), Naha-te and Tomari-te. At this time, it was common for the earliest masters to have studied under several different sensei and thus their training co-mingled various teachings into a more uniform mix of theories and techniques. Around the turn of the century, methods or systems of fighting began to evolve and become categorized as different ryu (styles)."[22]

McCarthy goes on to add, "By 1903, karate had more less become standardized into these ryu, many of which are still being taught today."[23] It is also interesting to note that Bishop indicates that many modern styles were introduced after World War II by Okinawans who saw the commercial value of claiming a unique style.[24] Much of what was taught to American service men immediately after World War II fell into this category.

In other cities, other prominent karate masters flourished and taught their art during the latter part of the 19th century. In addition to those teaching in and associated with the karate from Shuri, there were noted teachers in both Tomari and Naha. Tomari-te was very similar to Shuri-te but was reportedly taught under tight secrecy. However, several important Tomari-te masters need to be included in this investigation.

The dominant masters who taught in Tomari were Kosaku Matsumora and Kokan Oyadomari. Both of these early masters learned from Chinese instructors and had ties to Chinese methods. Kosaku Matsumora (1829-1898) learned Chinese boxing from a Chinese military attache living in Tomari named Ason. Kokan Oyadamori is also believed to have learned from a Chinese practitioner living in Tomari (perhaps Ason). Oyakamori practiced a light style that became the unique family system. As a style tomari-te was described as soft and not jerky.[25] Again we see the early masters practicing what seems to be identifiably a Chinese system of self-defense consisting of light, mobile movements.

Meanwhile, in Naha there was another group teaching karate of a similar nature but different enough to be called Naha-te. Primary among this group was Kanryo Higaonna (1853 - 1917). Higaonna was to Naha what Itosu is to Shuri. In his own way, Higaonna is one of the most influential karateka of his time. Some sources state that Higaonna trained under Arakai Seisho starting at age 20. Juhatsu Kyoda (one of Higaonna's top students) reported that Higaonna traveled to Fuchou several times to study Chinese boxing. In China, Higaonna's instructors are reported to have been either Ryu Ryo Ko and/or Wan Shin Zan. According to Juhatsu Kyoda, Higaonna learned from someone named Ru Ru (probably the same person as Ryu Ryo Ko).[26] While there seems to be some confusion about the specifics, the indisputable fact is that Higaonna trained under Chinese masters and practiced Chinese methods. Higaonna called his style of karate Shorei-ryu, which is often translated by Westerners today as "Enlightened Spirit School". However, it is speculated that Higaonna's use of the term Shorei actually was a reflection of the fact that he practiced a form of southern shoalin-tsu which he had learned in the Fuchou area of China.[27] From history, Higaonna's shorei-ryu (more likely read shaolin)or naha-te is reported to have been much lighter, softer and full of evasions than the karate developed after Higaonna's death by one of his top students, Chojun Miyagi.[28] As Bishop puts it "Higaonna's sparring was described by Nakaima as 'light with extraordinary footwork and low, fast kicks.' Thus, the foot anchoring, solid stances of modern Goju-ryu stand in contrast to Higaonna's style and it seems likely that, like many teachers of his time, he held much back when teaching fighting techniques."[29]

Thus far all of the most prominent names associated with the art of karate appear to have practiced an art based very closely on various chuan-fa styles. These include Sakugawa, Higaonna, Matsumora and Matsumura who lived during the 18th and 19th centuries and practiced *tode* or karate (China hand) in one form or another. Though they were closely tied to Chinese methods they retained their Okinawan background which gave their martial art a certain uniqueness.

It is curious to note that one distinction some historians attempt to build between chuan-fa and karate is the use of the closed fist. Haines claims *tode* is considered indigenous to Okinawa because it uses the closed fist techniques while true chuan-fa uses the open hand.[30] But as mentioned earlier, several

Chinese systems utilize the closed fist including Hsing Yi[31], and Choy Li Fut.[32] Even the Chinese exercise system known as Eight Brocades includes the closed fist.[33] Therefore, this distinction seems more artificial than factual and will not be included in the discussion.

As karate moved into the 20th century, the teachers changed. The group of 19th century masters, Higaonna et al, gave way to their students who formed the next group of masters. They included Kyan, Chibana, Miyagi, Motobu, and Funakoshi. Along with others, these men became the instructors who carried karate across the turn of the century into the 1900s. At this point Okinawa was nationally aligned with Japan so it is not unexpected to find that the new masters reflect a lower level of Chinese influence. Some of these masters did have limited exposure to Chinese teachers but to a lesser degree than previous karate masters. This change in the level of Chinese influence is in part responsible for the changes that karate was experiencing.

As noted earlier, it was this new group of instructors who authored and authenticated the change of the ideograph to read "kara" meaning empty instead of "kara" meaning China. McCarthy states that Hanashiro Chomo was the first to use the new ideograph in 1905. Karate had *do* added to the term and this new combined ideograph was officially accepted by the Japanese in 1933 and by Okinawa in 1936.[34] Haines states that Chomo first used "kara" meaning empty in his book titled Karate Soshu Hen in 1906.[35]

Not only had the ideograph used to designate karate changed, but the karate being taught had changed as well. Many

Okinawan masters were working for the acceptance of karate as an art by the Japanese. Because of this, many of the changes resulted from demands by the Dai Nippon Budoku Kai, which was the governing body for martial arts at that time. This was driven by the Japanese military society's idea of what was considered a *budo*.[36]

McCarthy states that the Butoku Kai placed certain requirements on karate in order for it to be accepted as an art, ". . . karate had to unify its many factions; the ideogram "karate" had to be changed to eliminate any Chinese connotations; karate groups had to adopt a standard practice uniform, establish a curriculum and standards for testing, assign degrees of proficiency, and organize a competition format like that of kendo and judo."[37] It is significant that it was this later generation of karate masters who had less direct contact with the Chinese martial arts that changed karate. Combat effective self-defense became less evident and karate became a means to train young men in physical conditioning and discipline. As shown earlier, Itosu began the change by modifying karate to allow the teaching of it in Okinawan schools. Also, as karate was incorporated into the Japanese military methodology, the training methods were modified so that training could accommodate larger numbers of students rather than the few individuals given special attention from earlier masters.

Another unique precept that was handed down by the masters of the early 20th century, especially Funakoshi, was the idea that karate was intended to be used as a defensive martial art. The inscription on Funakoshi's grave stone, quoted by Nagamine, is an important indication of the depth to which this ideal was at the heart of karate. The phrase "karate ni sente nashi (there is no first attack in karate)"[38] has been carried through several generations of karateka.

After the war, the leadership of karate transferred to the modern masters, those of the mid and late 20th century, including Nagamine, Higa, Miyazato, and Zenryo Shimabukuro. While many of these masters were trained in classical karate, few trained with multiple masters nor in multiple styles. Fewer still trained with Chinese instructors so the direct Chinese influence was largely lost. In addition, the influence of the changes made to karate by Itosu and in response to the Japanese demands cannot be entirely dismissed.

It was this later 20th century group who brought karate to the attention of the rest of the world. The karate they exemplified, however, was certainly different from the karate of the late 19th century. And more changes were taking place. With the rise of tournaments and tournament style karate, the art was becoming more oriented towards competition. Nagamine refers to the All-Japan Tournament held December 1, 1963 as a highlight of tournaments.[39] This drive to win tournaments, to gain fame and fortune, affected the karate itself. Rules eliminated many of the deadliest techniques and targets. Tournaments led to a rise in showmanship, in seeking the flashy, the artistic. More and more the self-defense aspects that had dominated karate during earlier eras were left out. For many, karate had now become a sport.

At the present time, the clock has moved full circle. While many traditional Okinawan systems have retained the heritage of karate as a self-defense, many western masters are researching the methods of earlier karateka, especially those before the turn of the century. They are seeking information on the ways more closely tied to the Chinese arts and to practical self-defense techniques. Recreations of old styles are surfacing that are designed to capture the old ways. Kyusho Justsu and Koryu Uchinadi are examples of disciplines where the knowledge of early methods of combat self-defense are resurfacing. Coupled with many other modern styles, today's karateka are exploring the roots of karate as a combat art. They are attempting to re-educate and revitalize the ancient self-defense art of karate especially in the western martial arts community.

It is apparent that karate has gone through several changes over the last 200 years. The changes correspond to different eras and different masters. The earliest Okinawan masters were Chinese trained. They practiced various systems of chuan-fa with some influence from Okinawan *te*. It is almost certain that the first generation of Okinawans (such as Matsumura and Higaonna) were practitioners of these Chinese martial arts. Some references conclude that karate came from Southern Shaolin boxing systems such as white crane (pai-huo-chuan), monk fist (luo-hau-chuan), intellectual fist (hsing-yi) and 8-triagrams (pa kua chuan).[40] Which Chinese systems directly influenced the formation of karate is not of major consequence; more important is the general nature of these Chinese systems. Most of them contain numerous grappling techniques. Grappling is clearly shown in the illustrations found in the *Bubishi*. However, many of these techniques appear to have been pushed aside as karate slowly evolved away from the older chuan-fa styles. Nagamine suggests that " Not until the late 17th and early 18th century did the art of karate take shape as *te* merged with the Chinese style of self-defense to form the present-day kata of karate."[41] *Te* and chuan-fa are both generally light, airy systems (though various systems of chuan-fa exhibit wide ranges of mobility) heavily integrated with grappling, throwing and striking. Later generations transformed these systems into the more Okinawan art of karate, and as can be seen in Choki Motobu's book, very few grappling techniques are evident. In many circles, karate as practiced in the 20th century, is more rigid and powerful, and is built, at least at lower levels, almost exclusively on impact techniques. Itosu was a primary influence on this change and for better or worse it seems certain that impact techniques are, and have been for a long time, key elements of karate. Karate training relies heavily on the makiwara which does not exist within chuan-fa unless one includes the Wing Chun dummy. Thus, one can conclude that karate has moved from a clearly Chinese system, to a self-defense system based on powerful impact techniques, to a modern sport karate and back to self-defense based on Chinese methodology. The art has completed the circle and returned to its roots.

But when did this martial art called karate come into being? If the birth of karate is based solely on the time when the ideograph became karate (empty hand), it is fairly clear that karate originated somewhere near the turn of the century even though it did not "officially" get recognized until early in the 20th century. Even then, it is evident that karate included several different dominant strategies. Light airy, evasive systems are just as much karate as the hard, immobile, powerful styles. In fact, often both of these general categories of karate co-existed. Still, the search is for a single definition of karate that will include all its various aspects.

Before a definition can be determined, it is imperative that the reasons for these changes to karate are explored. Otherwise, both the definition and doctrine established may be based on individual preferences and not on underlying principles. For one thing, it can easily be seen that lure of money spawned hype, styles, and in some cases, false information that would attract students - paying students. Tournaments were and continue to be driven by the promise of cash. Curriculums change to match the market perception of need. If students want to learn about self-defense, the commercial side of karate becomes focused on self-defense. Often, the advertisement is more hype about having developed the "ultimate self-defense" than any uniquely effective self-defense system. These conditions spawn charlatans who clutter the literature with unsubstantiated claims and false information. Therefore, legitimate research needs to weed out these theories, instructors, arts and styles from the arena of informed knowledge.

Others suggest that karate evolved because students were not completely trained before being released from their master's tutelage. Some authors have suggested that karate was originally a complete art which lost much of its original content because students never completed their training before they went off to train others.[42] Nagamine mentions the "instant instructor" as the source of much misinformation about karate after World War II.[43] A large body of evidence indicates that many Westerners received just such training either because they returned home too soon to be completely trained or because they were taken in by these lesser trained instructors. Nonetheless, it is the acknowledged oriental masters that are considered in this research so it is less likely that conclusions will be based on the opinions and methods of untrained karateka.

Though the idea that later masters were insufficiently trained in many of the details of karate methodology is plausible, there are other more compelling possibilities. One is that many of the best teachers were lost during the war. In addition, the younger generation of Okinawan or Japanese masters who began to teach karate after World War II may have been infatuated with the tournament aspects of karate which included the projected image of power. They neglected other aspects and centered their training around this narrower portion of the overall art of karate. This can be understood and may even be mirrored by similar circumstances that have overtaken American karate. In America, as in other parts of the world, the quest for tournament trophies has transformed karate into something more flashy than practical in less than thirty years. Many now see the pendulum swinging back. Those who only fifteen years ago were looking for a special, modified kata to "wow" the tournament judges are now searching for the best self-defense techniques that are contained within the most traditional karate kata that can be found. Is it then unreasonable to believe that the same thing happened on Okinawa? Perhaps the drive to win tournaments overshadowed the essence of karate as it was originally formulated. It may be that Itosu's demand that karate be powerful, immobile and impenetrable, captured the thoughts of the karateka of that time. It may also be that karateka and the students who flocked to pay the tuition demanded powerful techniques, "macho" karate, so to speak.

Possibly another more important clue as to why karate was transformed from the more inclusive Chinese systems into the impact-dominated system of later styles, may come from Seitoku Higa who is quoted by Bishop as saying "Unlike karate katas, *ti* (alternate spelling for *te*) takes a long time to master."[44] This admission that *ti*, full of grappling techniques, was hard for beginners to become competent in may be a clue as to why karate separated from its roots in chuan-fa and te.

Why the shift came about may never be satisfactorily answered. The significant question pertinent to the definition for karate is whether karate is an "impact" art, or whether it was formulated around many types of techniques, including grappling, throws, chokes and various other eclectic methods. As concluded earlier, karate is actually an art developed from chuan-fa and therefore must have originally included numerous types of techniques. Whatever the reason, the facts seem clear.

Karate underwent a transformation early in the 20th century, giving up much of the soft, light airy feel that had dominated the systems based more closely on the Chinese arts. It took on its own aura of power, of crushing opponents with a single blow. A major contributor to this revised thinking had to be the influential master Ankoh Itosu. At the same time, it became a more universally taught system, being introduced into the schools and embarking on the path of sport competition. These changes really define the beginnings of karate as we know it. Yet, if the essence of combat effective self-defense is to remain within the scope of karate, then the older, serious techniques must be included as part of the system.

So, how is karate defined? Bishop states that all karate is based on chuan-fa styles from the Foucho area[45] and evidence supports this theory. Ken Tallack in his preface to Choki Motobu's book says karate came from Shuri guardsmen who combined kata, makiwara and kumite training with the goal of "one blow, one life."[46] There seems to be some truth to this argument since several of the early masters were indeed Shuri guardsmen at one time or another during their lifespan. But are these two definitions mutually exclusive? Both indicate that the basis for karate is the combination of chuan-fa and *te*. Seen this way, the evolution of karate may reflect more of a change in focus than the creation of different arts. Karate, like most things, has not been static. Changes that karate has undergone since its inception are a reflection of the focus and the changes that each succeeding generation of karate teachers emphasized.

A perfect example of this change in focus is Miyagi's system of goju that is an adaptaion of Higaonna's shorei-ryu. Miyagi's goju is reported as more rigid and powerful than the Chinese-based system that was practiced by his sensei. Japanese goju may be even more removed from Higaonna's style. And yet, all of these are surely karate. So, it seems there are many definitions based on the specific time periods used to define karate. The goal here is to find a simplified definition broad enough to encompass all the various aspects of karate, past, present and future, and still provide a basis for separating karate from other arts. Several recurring aspects are evident. At least at initial training levels, karate is an impact art. It also includes various grappling techniques. In general, impact techniques are taught first and other broad categories of techniques are added as the karateka becomes more efficient at self-defense. If all this is wrapped into a single definition for karate it becomes: <u>Karate is an unarmed, individual self-defense developed in Okinawa sometime during the end of the 19th century that uses powerful impact techniques delivered by the hands (either open handed or closed fist), feet, elbows, knees or head to disable the attacker. Grappling techniques and other eclectic methods are added as the level of expertise of the karateka increases</u>. This definition contains the remnants of the Chinese systems and allows karate to retain its own flavor.

Having answered the first question, then what is the doctrine for this karate? If karate is a powerful weaponless art built on impact techniques, what was the doctrine that produced such an art out of the more grappling-oriented arts that preceded it? First, we must consider the goal of any martial art. In Nagamine's book, Ankichi Arakaki reportedly said karate originated from man's instinct for self-preservation.[47] The ultimate goal is, of course, survival. As noted earlier, karate deals with weaponless combat, witness the current kanji. But under what criteria does karate operate? As stated earlier, the origins of all the variations of karate come from the *jutsu*. Self-defense is the initial primary concern and the goal is survival. If the goal is survival, then it is imperative that the student becomes effective in defending oneself least the student die before learning the entire art. To that end we can define a secondary goal. Karate intends to produce the most effective self-defense possible for the minimum amount of training. In other words, the realistic self-defense goal is to be as good as possible as quickly as possible.

With this goal of karate as a guide, the search for the doctrine of karate recognizes other sources of information that served and guided early masters. One such book that predates even karate is the *Bubishi*. The *Bubishi* is known to have been used by the earliest karate masters including Higaonna, perhaps Sakugawa, and many modern masters including Funakoshi, Miyagi, Tatsuo Shimabukuro and Yamaguchi. In addition to specific self-defense techniques, the *Bubishi* contains the eight precepts of chuan-fa. These may be viewed as the umbrella doctrine that covers all the various armed and unarmed oriental combat systems. In capsule form these precepts are:

1) the mind is one with heaven and earth
2) circulation is like the sun and moon
3) inhaling is soft while exhaling is hard
4) adapt to change
5) react without thought
6) distance and posture will determine the outcome
7) see the unseen
8) expect the unexpected[48]

It is readily apparent that these precepts are very general. They can be applied to not only all the oriental martial arts but also to other combat systems as well. While this may be a good starting point, it does not directly lead us into the doctrine for karate. The precepts are too general and can even be applied to weapon arts as well as weaponless arts. They apply to grappling as readily as to impact arts. They do not explain what the unique doctrine for karate is.

Other authors have searched for answers about karate. Doctrine, as discussed by Forrest E. Morgan in his book *Living The Martial Way*, is the overlying theory that guides any martial art in setting the limits on activities, techniques and strategies. Doctrine refers to a set of broad general beliefs. Even so, to be useful as a doctrine for karate it cannot be as general as the precepts from the *Bubishi*. In the *Bubishi* the doctrine sought must refer to a system of personal combat, and for the art of karate it must apply to a specific system of weaponless personal combat. If the Bubishi gives us an idea for an umbrella doctrine for all arts, what is the specific doctrine for karate? As established earlier, the first statement from the definition for karate is that karate relies on the unarmed hands and feet. The doctrine must therefore start with the same premise and so the first statement within the doctrine must also be that karate is a martial art without weapons. Thus, karate is distinct from any form of armed combat.

What about the fact that for the beginner at least karate has discarded the grappling methods of other arts in favor of impact techniques. Why is this so? Many past masters have noted that the use of grappling takes a longer time to learn to reach a level of proficiency that makes it useful as a self-defense. There are numerous references indicating that masters of numerous weaponless combat arts have recognized the essential difference in training required to reach proficiency in impact versus grappling type arts. In the USKA Forum, December 1997, James S. Hanna quotes James Mitose from his book *What is Self-defense* as saying he "... advises readers to use punches, strikes and kicks when in desperate straits rather than grappling maneuvers" and in the same article, Hanna quotes Robert Smith from the book *Chinese Boxing* as saying ". . . striking is better than Chin-Na (Chinese grappling) unless the Chin-Na man is expert."[49] The conclusion, it seems, is that impact techniques take less time to learn than many grappling methods and students can produce effective results with less practice. Also, impact techniques have a higher probability of working in an actual self-defense situation so are less risky to use.

There are very good physiological reasons for this. Siddle discusses at length the classification of survival motor skills into gross, fine or complex.[50] To evaluate reaction under stress, the "inverted U" theory demonstrates that as stress increases, all three skill levels improve up to a point. At very high levels of stress, only gross motor skills remain capable and in fact, gross motor skills continue to improve even under levels of stress which make complex skills disappear. This explains why impact techniques are favored over other more complex skills for self-defense. In general, chin-na and many grappling skills fall within the complex motor skills classification. By contrast, karate's impact techniques generally fall into the gross motor skills category.

Siddle reports studies of law enforcement officers who overwhelmingly use gross motor skills in self-defense situations to the exclusion of other trained skills. The fact that stress management can overcome the effects of high stress levels no doubt explains why more complex self-defense systems can be effective but it also explains why they take a much longer training period.

In addition to the effects of stress, the increased level of complexity requires more training to make the techniques work in a combat situation. That, in and of itself, means the simpler techniques will be useful earlier in a martial artist's training. A simple block/punch self-defense is more easily learned and applied than a wrist lock which requires precise capture of the opponent's limb and manipulation of a joint or nerve point. Rather than take these conclusions without testing, an experiment was done with a dozen students at various levels of proficiency to see if it was easier to capture another's limb and manipulate it through some type of joint lock or grappling technique, or if a simple block and impact counterattack could be more quickly learned. Students were paired off with an *uke* and then attacked using simple punching or single-handed grabbing attacks. The defenders were instructed to either block and counter with an impact response or to ward off, grab the attacking arm and apply a grappling response. In all cases the verdict was that it was much easier to use the impact technique. The judgement was that grappling methods required more practice to be useful. Some students felt they might never have sufficient skill to make the grappling technique work against a determined, aggressive opponent. While this is a small sampling, it does demonstrate the relative ease of attaining an effective level between grappling, joint locking, etc. and the impact techniques that dominant karate.

Another way to evaluate this proposed doctrine is to study actual combat encounters. Individual combatants who are not employed in law enforcement were interviewed to determine the type of combat techniques used during actual physical violence. From their responses, it becomes evident that in a disproportionate number of instances impact techniques were used exclusively, even in cases where one or more of the combatants was trained in the grappling arts. Hitting is more effective and easier to apply (especially under stress), so it is used more often. Therefore, karate relies on training within this doctrine as a primary method. This does not mean that impact techniques are used exclusively, and more advanced students may include many other types of weaponless combat. As one gains skill in the impact techniques and achieves a level of self-defense competency, other more difficult techniques can be added to the repertoire. Once a student begins to have confidence in the ability to escape serious injury if attacked, he can begin to appreciate the need for techniques that allow for more limited defensive escalation. Grappling is a means to defend oneself with potential for less serious consequences for the attacker.

This information leads to the conclusion that karate depends, at least initially, on impact techniques and that there are good reasons for this. Thus, <u>the doctrine for karate is that it is a weaponless combat system based on the premise that impact techniques are more reliable and easier to learn than other techniques as a means of disabling an opponent</u>.

However, if the doctrine for karate is formulated simply around impact techniques, then the question might arise as to how karate is different from boxing, savate, or other percussion systems. Certainly, karate differs from any sport-oriented art in that it is based on the idea of "no rules" self-defense combat applications. In addition, the degree to which the karateka sets his or her expectations separates karate from other impact systems. Simple punches driven solely by physical strength are insufficient. Karate, as defined here, uses powerful techniques delivered by the hands, feet, elbows, knees or head and combines reaction force, breath/internal energy (chi or ki), strong postures, speed, timing and awareness and specific targeting to produce extraordinary results.

Several examples are available that demonstrate the effectiveness that karateka expect to achieve. Oyama reportedly defeated both a cow with seiken and a bull with shuto![51] Choki Motobu struck down a Russian traveling boxer with a single mae geri (or with a hand technique according to Nagamine[52]) at age 55.[53] Specific targets are a key consideration and the idea of the "one punch kill" is a training maxim.

This leads to another issue. Impact techniques landing on insensitive areas of the body have little effect and are wasted effort. Targeting and the effects impact techniques on the human body must be studied and therefore training must include utilization of specific targets. This will ensure that maximum results are obtained from minimum effort. This study of targeting is often referred to as kyusho-waza and is an important part of the doctrine of karate.

What doctrine covers this grand overview of karate? In succinct form, <u>the doctrine of karate seems to be that of a weaponless, impact system using specific targets for individual self-defense designed for immediate effectiveness that can be expanded to include other methods and varied techniques</u>.

What about the difference between the way (*do*) and combat practice or *jutsu*? Do these two karates have separate doctrines or could they retain the same one applied in different ways? Karatedo is the art of karate as a way for self-improvement, of seeking *shibumi*. Often this means severe physical and mental discipline, repetitious workouts that dull the mind and push the karateka into states of moving meditation. Karate-jutsu, on the other hand, deals only with pragmatic, useful self-defense geared toward physical combat.[54] If it works to disable the attacker, it is good. There is no need to worry about repetitions to perfect the precise form, movement, nor fluid grace that means so much within karatedo. Are they different arts? The *do* trains as if for *jutsu* without the specific intent nor the worry about actually using karate for self-defense. The *do* puts emphasis on the perfection of form while the *jutsu* focuses on results. Are these different methods for practicing the same art grounded in the same foundation? While it is true that emphasis on perfection can lose sight of the underlying self-defense principles, if karate is to remain the art being practiced, then self-defense should not be eliminated from the training. The purpose behind the techniques in either case needs to be effective self-defense. Therefore, there is no reason to search for different doctrines. The tools are the same. Only the workout methods and the slant given to various aspects of training are different. In short, *do* trains as if for jutsu without conscious intent to use the art in combat.

And now that a doctrine for karate has been proposed, the examples Morgan uses to explain doctrine need to be revisited. Morgan discusses the differences between tae kwan do and karate.[55] He claims they do not share a common doctrine since tae kwan do relies on the feet and uses a long-range doctrine while karate uses a short-range doctrine. Morgan says that tae kwon do proceeds on the assumption that legs are longer and stronger than arms and therefore, they should be the primary weapons. If the doctrine just established is accepted, then Morgan's argument appears to represent more of a difference in strategies. Various styles of karate may practice this same tae kwon do strategy, and many karateka within any style may practice either strategy. One says feet are more effective and should be the primary weapons. The other says that the hands are more effective and should be the primary weapons. It is also known that Northern and Southern Shaolin systems differ in a similar manner and yet it has never been stated that these are two different arts founded on different doctrines.[56] In short, both of these theories are different sides of the same coin. They do not define a doctrine, but only two strategies within the same doctrine.

It can be seen in many styles of karate that there is room for many particular, specific strategies. The doctrine for karate allows for, even encourages, many diverse strategies. This provides for various individual strategies for individual karateka. Often these personal strategies overlap, just as the strategies for various styles overlap under the umbrella doctrine for karate. This is not to be confused with the sport of tae kwon do nor sport karate. With either of these sports it is the rules that must be abided by. Therefore, the sport doctrine is artificially founded in the rules. Since rules have no direct relationship to combat self-defense situations, no sporting application can be considered a true self-defense martial art. Therefore, sports do not follow doctrines that apply to combat self-defense. Since karate is now defined as an unarmed self-defense, the doctrine that applies to karate is not the same as applies to the sport of karate.

<u>Conclusion</u>

The purpose of this paper was to answer the following questions: (1) How can karate be defined? (2) What is the doctrine or founding principles of karate? (3) Do the various manifestations of karate share a common doctrine? (4) Where does karate fit among the many different martial arts as a self-defense system?

Research shows that karate has existed in several separate eras and that it continues to evolve. Any definition of karate must acknowledge the existence of these variations throughout time. Fundamentally, karate is the practice of self-defense. The underlying factor that makes karate a unique or distinctive martial art is the relatively short period of training required to reach an effective level of self-defense skill. In general, less experienced karateka are more effective than similar levels of other arts because it is easier to learn to hit and kick than it is to grab, choke, throw or control an opponent. Considering all this, a case could be made for the existence of separate definitions and separate doctrines for each era of karate. In this paper, the conclusion is that **all** eras fall under the same definition and under one doctrine. The differences reflect only variations on the same theme.

At the very highest levels of mastery, karate includes both impact and grappling techniques though at different levels of proficiency than for other martial arts. This reflects the fact that at the highest levels of mastery, all unarmed, individual combat martial arts begin to lose their individual identity and become more and more alike. In the broadest sense, this is a result of the fact that there are only so many potential attacks that need to be defended. Therefore, as any given martial art reaches higher levels of mastery and begins to broaden the range of techniques used, the methods of response begin to converge on the same ones. When Nagamine said, "Even though we take different roads to ascend the wooded mountain, each of us can achieve our goal and appreciate the moon when we reach the top,"[57] he was talking about various styles of karate. But this idea applies just as well to a comparison of karate with other individual, weaponless martial arts. At the highest levels of mastery karate does encompass many different methods of self-defense. So watching the greatest masters may leave the impression that karate is indeed not a separate art. When examining the highest levels of mastery, it is not the top of the mountain where the trail has led that must be examined, it is the path by which the master got there that identifies the art the master practices. Karate provides a unique path to reach the upper levels of mastery.

Part of the doctrine established here is that karate teaches the easiest-to-learn techniques first to allow the student to achieve some level of effective self-defense in a short time. In line with this doctrine, it can be seen that much of karate training was designed around individual training. Karate training can be accomplished almost any time, anywhere, by any practitioner. In this respect, it differs from grappling because meaningful techniques can be practiced without reliance on a partner.

Since situations that demand the actual use of self-defense applications do not affect the average karateka, there is a definite need for other goals. This defines the need for karatedo. The goal for any martial art that wishes to be classified *do* remains perfection, perfection as it pertains to the human spirit. No one reaches perfection regardless of the length of training. For karatedo the real journey is a path inward and cannot be reached by perfection of technique alone. Karatedo indeed takes a lifetime. Thus, instead of spending a lifetime training for an attack that never materializes, the karateka can spend a lifetime refining and polishing character, will, patience, discipline and spirit. These goals have value for anyone and provide a sense of purpose that cannot be diminished by time, age, sex or physical condition.

Looking at both the definition and the doctrine, it must be concluded that all martial arts are roots of the same tree. Beginning with the *Bubishi*, there are certain underlying percepts that can be applied to every martial art. The most basic fundamental concept is the will to survive. Building on this general set of precepts, karate separates itself from the vast pool of martial arts first because it uses no weapons. It also is a system of individual self-defense combat. Then, based on the overwhelming evidence and opinions of the masters, it is concluded that karate is not as difficult to learn nor as complex to apply as the grappling arts. Once an effective level of self-defense mastery is attained, the doctrine of karate allows for other more complex training. The conclusion of some that karate is less sophisticated or that it is a lower level martial art than more complete (in the sense that it includes all the various methodologies for self-defense) arts such as jujitsu is wholly unfounded. For practical reasons, karate starts with the simplest techniques that can provide an effective means of self-defense. As mastery grows, karate embraces other categories of techniques and is only limited by the karateka's ability to learn, train and become proficient.

Specifically, then, the original questions are answered. First, the definition for karate is that karate is an unarmed, individual self-defense developed in Okinawa sometime during the end of the 19th century and that it uses powerful impact techniques delivered by the hands (either open handed or closed fist), feet, elbows, knees or head to disable the attacker. Grappling techniques and other eclectic methods are added as the level of expertise of the karateka increases.

Karate's doctrine states that karate is a weaponless, impact system using specific targets for individual self-defense designed for immediate effectiveness that can be expanded to include other methods and varied techniques.

The various manifestations of karate are all cut from the same cloth and therefore fall under a single doctrine. One exception is sport karate which uses rules in place of an established doctrine.

Finally, the conclusion is that karate does indeed exist as a separate martial art. Karate provides one of many paths to reach the summit of unarmed self-defense skill. Karate is not the only method available to reach this goal. Karate begins with a specific doctrine that guides the practitioner toward that goal. As the upper levels of mastery are attained, karate becomes melded with other systems of self-defense and differences are less obvious. However, it is the path to reach mastery that defines karate as a martial art, not the end of the journey. Karate is a martial art based on a doctrine that is translated through strategy and tactics into actual self-defense applications and training methods.

As a final note, one might look at how this definition and doctrine applies to a specific style of karate. As an example, Seito Shorei (the author's style) has, in fact, a style-specific doctrine which says to use the hands first and the feet second, to close with the attacker and, if possible, to get behind the attacker. Clearly, this is directly in line with the doctrine of karate beginning with the concept that the easiest to learn is the first to learn. It gives the student a degree of proficiency even while learning more advanced techniques. Also, Seito Shorei allows for personal strategies within the framework of the style in order to allow individual karateka to maximize their own abilities. Seito Shorei provides for the continuing expansion of each karateka's abilities, arsenal of techniques, and degree of mastery. Thus, Seito Shorei is an example of a style that provides a perfectly legitimate path to the mastery of self-defense using the doctrine of karate as its foundation. There is ample evidence that past masters developed and taught karate in this same manner.

The author hopes that instructors will now have answers to the questions that students ask about how to define karate, the doctrine of karate, and how is it different from other unarmed self-defense systems. As with any discipline of human endeavor, karate lies in the hands of those who are committed to seeking honest answers to just such questions and who are not afraid to face head-on whatever they find. Research that broadens the scope of knowledge for all karateka is essential to preserve the history and integrity of the martial art of karate.

The Hierarchy of Martial Theory

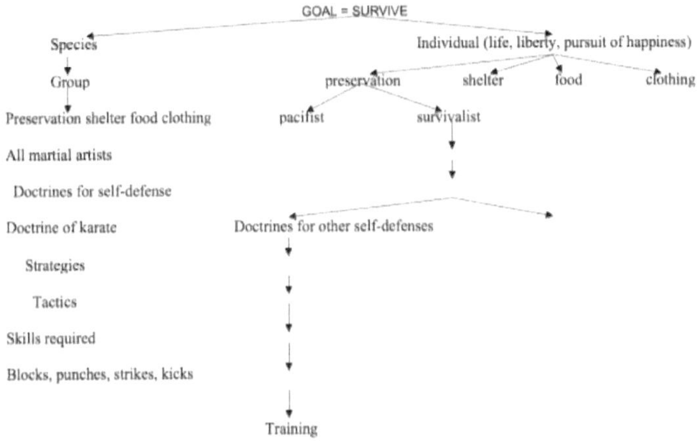

<u>End Notes</u>

1) Motobu, Choki, Okinawan Kempo, Masters Publications, Hamilton, Ontario, 1995 (actually, Tallack, Ken in his forward titled "Choki Motobu, a historical perspective," page 11)

2) Bishop, Mark, Okinawan Karate: Teachers, styles and secret techniques, A&C Black, Ltd., London, 1989, p. 10-11.

3) Lewis, Peter, The Martial Arts, Origins, Philosophy, Practice, Prion, London, 1996, p.19-20.

4) Funakoshi, Gichin, Karate-Do Kyohan, Kodansha International, Tokyo, 1973, p. 8

5) McCarthy, Patrick, The Bible of Karate Bubishi, Charles E. Tuttle Co., Rutland, VT, 1995, p., 34.

6) Bishop, Mark, Okinawan Karate: Teachers, styles and secret techniques, A&C Black, Ltd., London, 1989, p. 25-26.

7) Morris, Vince, Kyusho Secrets, copyright PMV Morris, 1996, p. 2.

8) Rench, Alan, Untitled, Unpublished notes from OSSKK Winter Seminar, 1997.

9) Morgan, Forrest E., Living the Martial Way, Barricade Books, Fort Lee, NJ, 1992, p. 36-40.

10) Haines, Bruce A., Karate's History and Traditions, Revised Edition, Charles E. Tuttle Co., Rutland, VT, 1995, p. 183.

11) Bishop, Mark, Okinawan Karate: Teachers, styles and secret techniques, A&C Black, Ltd., London, 1989, p. 11.

12) Haines, Bruce A., Karate's History and Traditions, Revised Edition, Charles E. Tuttle Co., Rutland, VT, 1995, p. 20.

13) Oyama, Masutatsu, What is Karate?, Japan Publications Trading Co., Rutland, VT, 1963, p. 18.

14) Nagamine, Shoshin, The Essence of Okinawan Karate-do, Charles E. Tuttle Co., Boston, 1976, p. 24.

15) McCarthy, Patrick, Beyond Physical Training, International Ryukyu Karate Research Society, Brisbane, Australia, 1994, p. 6.

16) McCarthy, Patrick, The Bible of Karate Bubishi, Charles E. Tuttle Co., Rutland, VT, 1995, p. 59.

17) ibid, p. 34.

18) Nagamine, Shoshin, The Essence of Okinawan Karate-do, Charles E. Tuttle Co., Boston, 1976, p. 20-21.

19) Haines, Bruce A., Karate's History and Traditions, Revised Edition, Charles E. Tuttle Co., Rutland, VT, 1995, p. 87.

20) Bishop, Mark, Okinawan Karate: Teachers, styles and secret techniques, A&C Black, Ltd., London, 1989, p.61.

21) Bishop, Mark, Okinawan Karate: Teachers, styles and secret techniques, A&C Black, Ltd., London, 1989, p.99.

22) McCarthy, Patrick, Classical Kata of Okinawan Karate, Ohara Publications, Inc., Santa Clarita, CA, 1987, p.18.

23) Ibid

24) Bishop, Mark, Okinawan Karate: Teachers, styles and secret techniques, A&C Black, Ltd., London, 1989, p.11.

25) Bishop, Mark, Okinawan Karate: Teachers, styles and secret techniques, A&C Black, Ltd., London, 1989, p.75.

26) Bishop, Mark, Okinawan Karate: Teachers, styles and secret techniques, A&C Black, Ltd., London, 1989, p.25-26.

27) Rench, Alan S. Shorei-Ryu: A Definitive Kyohan, Borealis Publications, Aurora, CO, 1996, p.533.

28) Bishop, Mark, Okinawan Karate: Teachers, styles and secret techniques, A&C Black, Ltd., London, 1989, p.26-27.

29) Bishop, Mark, Okinawan Karate: Teachers, styles and secret techniques, A&C Black, Ltd., London, 1989, p.27

30) Haines, Bruce A., Karate's History and Traditions, Revised Edition, Charles E. Tuttle Co., Rutland, VT, 1995, p. 91-92.

31) Jing-Ming, Yang and Shou-Yu, Liang, Hsing Yi Chuan, YMAA Publication Center, Jamaica Plain, MA, 1990, p. 88-113.

32) Hallander, Jane, The Complete Guide to Kung Fu Fighting Styles, Unique Publications, USA, 1985, p. 72-79.

33) Rench, Alan S. Shorei-Ryu: A Definitive Kyohan, Borealis Publications, Aurora, CO, 1996, p.401-413.

34) McCarthy, Patrick, The Bible of Karate Bubishi, Charles E. Tuttle Co., Rutland, VT, 1995, p. 56.

35) Haines, Bruce A., Karate's History and Traditions, Revised Edition, Charles E. Tuttle Co., Rutland, VT, 1995, p. 20.

36) McCarthy, Patrick, The Bible of Karate Bubishi, Charles E. Tuttle Co., Rutland, VT, 1995, p.56.

37) McCarthy, Patrick, Classical Kata of Okinawan Karate, Ohara Publications, Inc., Santa Clarita, CA, 1987, p.20.

38) Nagamine, Shoshin, The Essence of Okinawan Karate-do, Charles E. Tuttle Co., Boston, 1976, p. 13.

39) Nagamine, Shoshin, The Essence of Okinawan Karate-do, Charles E. Tuttle Co., Boston, 1976, p. 26.

40) Rench, Alan S. Shorei-Ryu: A Definitive Kyohan, Borealis Publications, Aurora, CO, 1996, p.533.

41) Nagamine, Shoshin, The Essence of Okinawan Karate-do, Charles E. Tuttle Co., Boston, 1976, p. 21.

42) Morris, Vince, Kyusho Secrets, copyright PMV Morris, 1996, p. 4-5.

43) Nagamine, Shoshin, The Essence of Okinawan Karate-do, Charles E. Tuttle Co., Boston, 1976, p. 25.

44) Bishop, Mark, Okinawan Karate: Teachers, styles and secret techniques, A&C Black, Ltd., London, 1989, p.165

45) Bishop, Mark, Okinawan Karate: Teachers, styles and secret techniques, A&C Black, Ltd., London, 1989, p.10.

46) Motobu, Choki, Okinawan Kempo, Masters Publications, Hamilton, Ontario, 1995 (actually, Tallack, Ken in his forward titled "Choki Motobu, a historical perspective," page 11)

47) Nagamine, Shoshin, The Essence of Okinawan Karate-do, Charles E. Tuttle Co., Boston, 1976, p. 37

48) McCarthy, Patrick, The Bible of Karate Bubishi, Charles E. Tuttle Co., Rutland, VT, 1995, p., 159-160.

49) Hanna, James S., USKA Forum, USKA Inc., Phoenix, AZ, Dec. 1997, p.15.

50) Siddle, Bruce K., Sharpening the Warrior's Edge, PPCT Research Publications, Millstadt, IL, 1996, p. 39-58.

51) Oyama, Masutatsu, What is Karate?, Japan Publications Trading Co., Rutland, VT, 1963, p. 118.

52) Nagamine, Shoshin, The Essence of Okinawan Karate-do, Charles E. Tuttle Co., Boston, 1976, p. 44.

53) Motobu, Choki, Okinawan Kempo, Masters Publications, Hamilton, Ontario, 1995 (actually, Tallack, Ken in his forward titled "Choki Motobu, a historical perspective," page 16)

54) McCarthy, Patrick, The Bible of Karate Bubishi, Charles E. Tuttle Co., Rutland, VT, 1995, p., 56.

55) Morgan, Forrest E., Living the Martial Way, Barricade Books, Fort Lee, NJ, 1992, p. 38-40.

56) Chow, David, and Spangler, Richard, Kung Fu, History, Philosophy and Techniques, Unique Publications, Burbank, CA, 1982, p. 39.

57) Nagamine, Shoshin, The Essence of Okinawan Karate-do, Charles E. Tuttle Co., Boston, 1976, p. 23.

Appendix A

Doctrine, Strategy, Tactics: Who Cares?
by James D. Brumbaugh

A tiger in the wild is an effective fighting machine known for power, speed and grace. And just as the tiger manifests certain attributes when pouncing on its prey, every martial artist displays recognizable characteristics in his/her specific martial art form. What separates man from tiger is the ability to analyze, question and categorize the world around him so as to better understand it. This is the reason that man formulates theories and opinions on his martial arts and the tiger does not.

In order to analyze and categorize our martial arts, we devise terms that allow us to separate various arts by representative characteristics. Three terms that have been used lately to describe defining aspects of the martial arts are doctrine, strategy and tactics. In his book, Living The Martial Way(1), Major Forrest E. Morgan suggests that understanding these terms and their relationship to any martial art is extremely important for us as warriors. If these terms are so important, then why are they seldom if ever mentioned in many martial arts dojos? Are they really all that important if our only goal is to learn and train in an art as *do* rather than *jutsu*? In many cases it seems that neither the students nor the instructor care. Maybe they don't need to care. Why worry about abstract issues like doctrine, strategy or tactics?

To answer these questions, we must start by asking what is doctrine, strategy and tactics? What do these terms have to do with the martial arts? We begin with the dictionary definitions of these three terms. Looking in Webster's (2) we find:

"doctrine - a particular principle, position or policy taught or advocated as of religion, government, etc."

"strategy - a plan, method or series of maneuvers or stratagems for obtaining a specific goal or result."

"tactic - a plan, procedure or expedient for promoting a desired end or result."

But these are sterile definitions established by common usage and are not easily related to the martial arts. In order to decide their importance, we must understand these terms within the scope of the martial arts. From these dictionary definitions we can develop meanings for doctrine, strategy and tactics that apply directly to the martial arts.

For the bugeisha, doctrine is a principle or policy taught or advocated as a martial art. It is, in fact, the high-level theory and philosophy that provides the framework within which any martial art functions. The doctrine for each martial art is usually established by that art's founder. Therefore, it may seem less important to those who are not trying to formulate a new art. But similar to the doctrine that guides a business by stating what product or service a business will provide, the doctrine for a martial art puts forth the theory of combat that dictates what methods that art will use. In its simplest form, doctrine selects the tools that a specific art will use. It is the guiding philosophy that dictates that the swordsman uses a sword while the karateka does not. It is the doctrine that establishes that the judoka uses throws, chokes and selected grappling techniques and not a myriad of other seemingly related techniques.

Strategy is the next step in the development of a martial art. It is the plan or method for obtaining a specific goal. Within the doctrine, there will be many possible plans that may work. Strategy is the theory of how to apply the principles set forth by each art's doctrine against various possible enemies. Strategy takes the selected weapons, the tools deemed appropriate by the founder, and plans for their use in actual combat. If the founder has not selectively excluded either offensive or defensive actions within the scope of the doctrine, then the strategies devised will fall into both offensive and defensive categories. Offensive and defensive strategies are like the left and right hand—used at the correct time, either will work but you must plan ahead to be able to recognize when that proper time is. As stated earlier, strategy will be devised so as to cover many possible enemies. Strategy will examine the possible weaknesses and strengths and devise plans for countering the opponent's strength and capitalizing on weaknesses. Strategy is the plan that connects the doctrine and the tactics. It evaluates ways in which to use the tools of the doctrine and makes plans for that use.

In the martial arts, tactics are the procedures and expedients to promote a desired end. For the martial artist, that desired end is usually survival or victory. In short, tactics are the intelligent acts of combat performed during aggressive confrontation that fulfill the theories of doctrine and the plans of strategy. Tactics can be as simple as a straight seiken tsuki to the face or as subtle as dodging and turning until the streetlight catches your opponent in the eyes and then delivering a seiken tsuki to the face. Individual tactics are the application of a martial art. Without tactics, self-defense becomes random acts that may or may not succeed based purely on chance. Tactics provide a way for the mind to guide the body in self-defense to increase the likelihood of success. Tactics are the actions required to fulfill the plans established by the strategy.

So, what's the difference between doctrine, strategy and tactics? The difference lies in the degree of specificity and the ratio of action to abstract thought. On the one hand, doctrine is general and theoretical. Doctrine selects the guiding principles from among all possible martial actions and narrows it to a manageable few. It does not spell out specific actions. Doctrine deals with concepts. Strategies take the doctrine and develop from it plans for applying general groups of physical actions against potential opponents. Tactics are the doing, the physical application of doctrine and strategy. Thus, it is that doctrine provides the framework for developing a strategy. Strategies are the plans around which the martial artist develops a set of tactics which in turn dictates the required skills for that art.

To the beginner, it can be difficult to look at any physical action and identify the guiding component from the doctrine or strategy that led to the formulation of that action. Once the beginner has selected a martial art to study, he is generally too busy to think about doctrine or strategy. The beginner starts at the bottom rung of the martial arts ladder, working to learn the specifics, the individual skills, the basic movements. At first, he practices the required skills until he can perform them spontaneously in accordance with the tactical goals even though these goals may not be spelled out by the instructor. As the martial artist progresses, he will reach a level where some strategies may be presented by the instructor. Often this is where the learning stops. It should not! This is where the advanced martial artist must push to gain a deeper knowledge, to understand the strategy and doctrine that led to the development of that martial art. In order to fully understand an art, it is necessary to understand that art as if you knew the mind of the founder, as if you were the founder. Knowing doctrine and strategy help provide that depth of knowledge for a martial art. They provide a look at the art as envisioned by the founder.

Except to help in the selection process, the beginner does not need to know the doctrine. On the other hand, the master must know it extremely well. Otherwise, how can the master understand the essence of his art? And how can the master teach others when he has not yet grasped the underlying foundation that was used to establish the art? If any martial art is to survive it must do so through the efforts of those who examine every aspect, understand the most minute details, and surely those who comprehend fully the doctrine, strategy and tactics. Individual actions without that foundation are merely Pavlovian responses to prearranged stimuli. They are not martial arts. And without doctrine, strategy and tactics, specific martial arts soon become lost arts.

References:

1) Morgan, Forrest E., Living the Martial Way,

2) Webster's New Universal Unabridged Dictionary, Barnes & Noble Books, New York, 1992.

Appendix B

Styles: Marketing Tool or the Foundation for Learning?
By James D. Brumbaugh

Much has been said about styles in karate and most of it has to do with being "better." But is one style of karate really any better? If not, why have styles at all?

As most people know styles of karate are a recent development. Karate during the antique era (pre-1900) was taught in small groups, often at the instructor's home without any connection to a "style." The masters from that era often trained under multiple instructors of various lineage mixing Okinawan, Chinese and Japanese arts. Students looked for instructors by name and reputation not by publicized style. Generally, the training was individualized to fit each student. Instructors taught only a few students with little commercial competition. Once commercial considerations came into play (especially after WWII), styles were recognized as an important marketing tool and were exploited. Thus, the emphasis on style sprang into prominence.

This commercial emphasis on styles has misled the public to think there is something significant about a style. Many prospective martial arts students enter a dojo and the first question they ask is "What style do you teach?" If you answer with a style name, they nod and go on to questions about price and hours of instruction. If you ask them about styles, it soon becomes apparent that often they know nothing about styles, only that they should ask the question.

Because we all evaluate others based on our own beliefs or experience, we tend to equate our style with superiority. We're proud of it, and probably should be. But this ethnocentrism reinforces unjustifiable attitudes about the importance of style.

Admittedly there are charlatans who have little expertise or teaching skills. They claim "mastery" in the "ultimate" martial art. They promise to make you invincible in 90 days! These "styles" are excluded from the discussion because their very advertised nature proclaims them less than authentic.

But what about the relative merits of the legitimate systems of learning where sufficient blood, sweat and even tears provide evidence that karate is being taught. Stepping back for a moment and forgetting which style we practice will allow for a more objective comparison. If we do that, we find that comparing karate systems reveals more similarities than differences. Every style is bound by the limits of the human anatomy. And at least on that point they all must be alike. Every karate style contains techniques based on impact methods often intertwined with grappling. They may use different training methods but the general skills learned are similar enough to be considered variations on the same theme. Styles may or may not include kumite, kata or partnered drills for training. They may be sport oriented, self-defense oriented, fitness oriented or self-improvement oriented. Even within the same style different dojo may have different emphasis. To the student, it is the emphasis of the training that is often more important than the style. Young adults will have different goals than retirees. Mature adults will be different than younger children. So, the training focus becomes a key issue. Therefore, how the training is conducted and what the expected outcome from the training is should be more important to the public and will depend more on the individual instructor than on the style.

If the training focus is more important than the style, maybe we should do away with styles. What real purpose do they serve? Education in any field has for centuries been most effectively accomplished by building a base of knowledge and skill then adding to it in a logically tiered manner. Karate is no different. A set curriculum, therefore, is necessary to structure a student's growth and to allow for consistent training from one student to the next. Since no one instructor can know all there is to know about self-defense or even karate as it applies to all individuals, the style provides the template for basic learning. How much is required and how the learning items are arranged within the progression forms the elements of each style. This becomes the specific body of knowledge that can be transferred from instructor to student to new student. It gives the training a sense of continuity. Thus, styles can be thought of as the equivalent of undergraduate and graduate studies in academic fields. Kyu material approximately equals the undergraduate area, the lower dan ranks are the graduate work and the upper dan ranks becomes the area left for individual concentration and/or the karateka's life's work.

Styles also provide a sense of historical continuity and can be used to pass on the lessons from previous instructors. This helps many students feel they belong to something bigger than themselves, to a community that extends into the past and reaches into the future. This sense of heritage fulfills a basic human need and should not be underestimated.

On the other hand, styles can be too restrictive. They should not be so regimented that they suppress freedom of expression.

Each student has different strengths and weaknesses. Styles should leave room for individualized learning. In many cases this will necessitate providing ways to cross-train between styles or other martial arts. Instructors and the style precepts should allow and encourage the exchange of ideas with other styles and martial arts instructors. While this may seem suicidal to those trying to run a commercial dojo it only means you need to give your students quality instruction and pay attention to their needs as students. This includes opening doors to knowledge outside the style. In the long run you will retain more of your better students who won't have to leave when they find some other aspect of the martial arts grabs their interest.

Within this concept, it becomes imperative that instructors openly explain to their students that any single system does not contain all there is to know about karate, not even the style they are studying. As students progress in rank, they should be required to increase their knowledge base and at the same time individualize their training to best fit their own strengths, weaknesses and individual goals. As students expand their knowledge, they should also be expected to improve the skill sets contained within the style. This begins to build the notion that higher-ranking students are expected to grow, not stagnate. Students who stop growing and learning will soon get bored and find other interests. Without the highest-level students, the style will die anyway. So, in order to keep students learning, the bar must continually be set higher. To continue to grow they will need to learn more about the basics within their system, variations presented by other systems and strategies that best fit their needs. They will need a more complete understanding of each and every aspect within their karate and how it fits within the grand scheme of martial arts. This cannot happen without allowing access to the outside world.

Growth, therefore, must be on two levels. First, the core material of the style must continuously be improved, re-internalized and more fully explored. Second the student must gain knowledge, skill and competency in areas related to but outside the style's core material, areas that the student chooses for themselves.

The style's established curriculum needs to remain the constant underpinning for all advanced training. One objection is the fear that the style will become so diluted that it ceases to be a style. To avoid this, it is imperative that students specifically know what is and what isn't part of the style. If they will learn the style, they will know what it is, but they will know more about how the style fits in to the bigger picture of martial arts in general. They will be better karateka.

Styles provide the structure to ensure a stable foundation and methodology for learning. But the style is not the "end-all be-all;" it's only a foundation for further learning. Appreciate all worthy styles and don't be too harsh judging them! Enjoy seeing and learning about both the differences and similarities. At the same time, as an instructor, demand continual improvement in core skills and keep an open mind to allow for individual growth and cross training. This will make for the best karate in the long run.

Appendix C

The Mind and the Martial Artist
By James D. Brumbaugh

Often only the physical aspects of martial arts training get any attention, especially from those who have not studied any martial art for an extended period of time. It is the punches, kicks, arm locks, and throws that are viewed as the essence of these seemingly mysterious pursuits. In truth, the dedicated martial artist trains both the body and the mind. With experience and breadth of knowledge, it becomes apparent that without training the mind and establishing a link between mind and body, there are no true martial arts.

But gaining that connection between mind and body is neither straight forward nor simple. From the Oriental perspective, we are of two minds; the intellectual mind and the emotional mind. This concept mirrors the Occidental view that we can think with our mind or our heart. Perhaps a medical professional would ascribe that notion to different parts of the brain where the thinking takes place. Regardless of the perspective, the fact is that we do respond to our surroundings generally in two ways: intellectually and/or emotionally.

How does that relate to the martial arts and what can be done to improve our responses to situations that confront us? First, it is important for the martial artist to understand both the intellectual and emotional factors and how they might be useful or counterproductive.

When a flight-or-fight situation arises, it is imperative to utilize both "brains". The emotional mind brings the adrenaline rush that provides an extra surge of energy, increased strength, and dulls pain. All of these aspects are necessary for self-defense. However, allowed to get out of control, cognition and fine motor skills disappear along with much of the training that is required to escape from the situation. This is where the intellectual mind must keep the emotional mind in check, drawing the best parts from the emotional rage without succumbing to it.

Controlling breathing is one way to maintain control over emotional reaction and it is one way martial artists train themselves against negative physiological effects even though they cannot create the same stress levels in training that will be encountered during a real life confrontation.

Another important aspect of mental training is the concept of intent. Intent is a measure of the actual outcome the martial artist wants to occur. Hurting another person is not something that comes naturally to most people, sociopaths excluded, and so the willingness to do harm is a personal decision for each individual. That decision must be made ahead of time. Otherwise, the mind will debate the moral aspects of various options at the very moment when action is needed. If there is any hesitation then it will be too late.

Having said all that, there is another more important mental aspect to the martial arts. The best mental state during fight-or-flight situations is a blank mind, one that sees everything and allows unimpeded reactions without rational internal debate. "Mind like water" is a common saying around martial arts dojo (training hall). Water reflects everything around it without making judgments or drawing conclusions. This way the mind does not interfere with the reflex responses built up over long periods of training. It also prevents the mind from pre-planning a course of action before the situation has developed to the point where action is needed. Reacting too soon can lead to disaster. It's almost as if you need to take the conscious mind out of the equation to maximize speed, training and efficiency. Some of the best responses result from an empty mind almost as if by magic, without conscious thought or plan. They just happen.

How can you train for mental control during times of conflict when you cannot duplicate the stress found in real life? Meditation, chi kung, breathing exercises, sanchin (breathing and tension) kata and often kumite are useful in improving mental controls. Included in this training is learning to ignore pain from the injuries that will almost certainly occur.

One standard meditation technique that is used by many martial artists is to sit quietly, and concentrate consciously on relaxing individual muscles until the entire body has released tensions. When that begins to come naturally without conscious thought, transfer the focus to the breath. In, out, breathing with the diaphragm and pulling air all the way to the bottom of the lungs. After that becomes automatic, the next phase often is to work on chi (internal energy) circulation exercises, of which there are many. Lead the chi with the mind through the body much like a stream follows a creek channel.

Ultimately, the mind and body will be in tune. The mind will become calm in all circumstances, without prejudice or conscious thought and will guide the martial artist intuitively to the best course of action even as it allows the body to react exactly as needed.

Don't miss out!

Visit the website below and you can sign up to receive emails whenever James Brumbaugh publishes a new book. There's no charge and no obligation.

https://books2read.com/r/B-A-MDC-QDLOC

BOOKS 2 READ

Connecting independent readers to independent writers.

About the Author

James Brumbaugh lives in northeast Ohio where he spends his time writing sci-fi, fantasy and suspense novels, training at karate, building a Japanese garden in his back yard, and taking walks in the local metro parks. He has spent more than sixty years studying various martial arts, the last thirty focused on Shorei-ryu karate, eventually attaining the rank of hachi-dan. He continues to mentor others on their karate journey.